THAMES

An Anthology of River Poems

THAMES

An Anthology of River Poems

Compiled by

Anna Adams

with a preface by

Iain Sinclair

Etchings by James McNeill Whistler

London
ENITHARMON PRESS
1999

First published in 1999
by the Enitharmon Press
36 St George's Avenue
London N7 0HD

Distributed by Littlehampton Book Services
through Signature Book Representation
2 Little Peter Street
Manchester M15 4PS

ISBN 1 900564 46 7

British Library Cataloguing-in-Publication Data.
A catalogue record for this book is available
from the British Library.

Set in 10.5pt Bembo by Bryan Williamson, Frome,
and printed in Great Britain by
The Cromwell Press, Wiltshire

CONTENTS

WHISTLER'S ETCHINGS IN THE TEXT

RIVER OF GHOSTS

The river that is blood is time; sweeping its circuit, never completed, source to sea, through *Finnegans Wake*. Joyce feminised the Liffey: 'Anna was, Livia is, Plurabelle's to be.' A true writer, coerced shaman, filters and echoes all the voices, living and dead, the elements of breath and language.

But the Thames is an older, darker beast, serpentine and subtle; a working river queening it over its subdued tributaries – Colne, Falcon, Peck, Westbourne, Tyburn, Walbrook. Its colour is not the lurid ceramic blue of computer-enhanced Millennium Dome prospectuses, nor the vivid lycra-green of the *EastEnders* credit sequence. Colour is sediment, a mud poultice; crocodile khaki. 'The river's tent is broken'. Weatherproofed canvas. A drowned vagrant's raincoat. Deleted memory files.

Thomas Gray's mistakenly sexed and personalised 'Father Thames' doesn't owe allegiance to any one poet. The river is the essence of the great poem of the city; constant, changeable, sluggish and swift. Poets who recognise this will not waste their gifts on an unrequired flirtation. The Thames can never be a sidebar to the picaresque. A shuffle of limpid views and provocation for small gasps at localised performances of the transcendent.

Any decent anthology of river poems will soon disclose a process of reverse alchemy – from Spenser's 'silver-streaming Thames', through Pope's 'sun-beams trembling on the floating tides', to our contemporary lead-coloured drift. It's not the tides that have changed but our way of seeing them. Gilded scintillae flashing on wavecrests merge into the fire sermons of Ludwig Meidner and Oskar Kokoschka. A vortex of tumbling buildings and burning water. A spirit fiercely translated by the British apocalyptics: David Gascoyne (who grew up in Twickenham), Dylan Thomas and George Barker. Barker, as Allen Ginsberg recalled, made a link, a chemical connection, to William Blake (who lived within sight of the river in Lambeth). 'It was Sunday the 12th of April I saw / The figure of William Blake,' Barker writes in *Calamiterror*, 'bright and huge / Hung over the Thames at Sonning.'

Anna Adams in her gathering makes proper reference to the great central lineage of Thames poets: Spenser, Pope, Blake. A genealogy leading, for the present time, to Eliot's *The Waste Land*, where previous voices break through an anxious schizophrenic surface. There is no easy conclusion to this story. From the fire bomb that chipped Cleopatra's Needle in the First War to the squadrons of bombers using the river as a flight path in the Blitz, the Thames has resisted its disguise as a prospect to be colonised by Canaletto's successors, prescriptive architects and predatory planners.

There is room in *Thames* for occasions of elevated tourism such as Wordsworth's ecstatic seizure on Westminster Bridge. And for moments when the charm of the particular finds a voice. I miss a sequence that is key to my own understanding of London mythology, 'The Lady of the Pool' from David Jones's *The Anathemata*.

> Coming up on a spring tide
> with her Rotherhithe mate and her Limehouse skipper and a
> Sittingbourne bred pilot in her conning-house

But this anthology will have done its job if it ferries us back to the power of the river and the songs it has provoked. The Thames was never a feature to be dressed up or tricked out with new toys. It's not a backdrop or decorated screen, but the means by which a city was founded, established, led towards prosperity; a show and pride of wealth before an interesting cycle of decline.

IAIN SINCLAIR

'A STRONG BROWN GOD' – FOREWORD

> I do not know much about gods; but I think that the river
> Is a strong brown god –

The title of this foreword comes from 'The Dry Salvages', and refers to an American river known to T. S. Eliot: yet Eliot's lines also fit our Thames, which is, or was

> sullen, untamed and intractable,
> Patient to some degree, at first recognised as a frontier;
> Useful, untrustworthy, as a conveyor of commerce;
> Then only a problem confronting the builder of bridges.
> The problem once solved, the brown god is almost forgotten
> By the dwellers in cities . . .

That Londoners have tended to ignore their river was proved to me when I began hunting out poems in celebration of the Thames. Since I was somewhat in love with the river myself, I was at first surprised that there were not more of them, for its banks have harboured poets since Geoffrey Chaucer was born in Thames Street, London, about 1343, thirty years after his mentor Boccaccio was born in Florence. In middle life the acknowledged fountain-head of English poetry is thought to have been living at Greenwich, and having been appointed Clerk of the King's Works by Richard II in 1389, he was put in charge of the construction and repair of walls and ditches for the marshes between Greenwich and Woolwich. Yet, though close to and concerned with the Thames, Chaucer did not write about it. The Canterbury Pilgrims met at Southwark, but none of them remarked on the state of the tide.

So Londoners were already taking the Thames for granted, as if it were a parent, but the river has, nevertheless, been written about by one or two poets every century since the fifteenth, so the poems I have found form together a murmuring river. This river changes as it flows through Spenser's fresh fields towards ever-growing towns into an overcast cityscape that stinks more and more of industry, effluent and poverty. Its surface reflects history: the flattery of courtiers, the Great Fire of London and London's rebuilding; the growth of Empire, the corruption of the old order and the urban squalor of Blake's day.

In the late nineteenth century, William Morris wrote:

> Forget six counties overhung with smoke,
> Forget the snorting steam and piston stroke,
> Forget the spreading of the hideous town;
> Think rather of the packhorse on the down,
> And dream of London small and white and clean,
> The clear Thames bordered by its garden green.

And Morris had much to say about an idealised Thames in the prose of *News from Nowhere*, and perhaps something of his should have been included whole. Geoffrey Grigson has said that Morris wrote like the Thames. He certainly lived beside it, at Hammersmith and also up-river in the country, and journeyed up and down and took great pleasure in it. But, being impatient of earthly paradises, I chose to occupy several pages with the eighteen-year-old Charles Hamilton Sorley's symbolic river instead. This, though unnamed, resembles the Thames, and is so prescient of the Great War, and his own death in that war, aged twenty, that I felt – partly because of the poem's immaturity – that it spoke for his generation.

I have been able to represent the major First World War poet, Wilfred Owen, by an untypical short lyric, 'Shadwell Stair'. In this the poetry is not in the pity but in the near-melodrama. It is also in the poetry, and its evocation of a smoky, gaslit London.

Thomas Hardy's poem, 'A Wife in London', was written during the Boer War, and is, like most poetry, primarily about human beings. Its heroine is a dweller on Thames' banks, and the sad story it tells has a misty, rivery atmosphere. Francis Thompson's religious poem, 'In No Strange Land', culminates in Christ walking on the waters of the Thames, while Alice Meynell's 'The Visiting Sea' is really more sexual than topographical, but, as Meynell was a Londoner, she probably learned about tides from the Thames.

As the river of poems arranged itself in near-chronological order, its continuity was proved to me by the entire lines that have washed down, like green branches from an upriver tree, from Spenser's 'Prothalamion' to lodge in the polluted banks of Eliot's *Waste Land* river from which, the poet laments, the nymphs have departed.

Now that our century is all but over, and even Eliot is becoming historical, we treat the river with a little more respect, and have even gone so far as to present it with a necklace, the Thames Barrage, hoping thereby to keep it under control. This suggests that, since we have woken up to the fact of global warming, we have begun to fear the unruly brown god again.

The honest realism of contemporary poets is a very hopeful thing. This is what life is like, they say, as men and women speaking to men and women: Andrew Motion gives us his vivid sightings of the Thames, from its grassy source, through Oxford, to the London Embankment; and he also commemorates a friend who drowned in the *Marchioness*. John Greening records having grown up by the Thames, west of London, in an elongated, river-shaped poem that becomes almost a love poem and manages to end with an evocative reference to the 'silent / longing and searching of Isis.'

Ursula Fanthorpe names the London tributaries of the Thames, as is fitting, for women have been the nameless tributaries of poetry for long enough; then she relates these underground rivers to those older, deeper rivers – Phlegethon, Acheron, Lethe, Styx – that run through all poetry, whatever its theme.

When I began to think this anthology complete, with twelve poems from before 1900 and twelve twentieth-century poems, I allowed myself to advertise it a little, with the result that a flock of suggestions came winging in so that now there are thirty-three poems and the pivotal point has become T. S. Eliot's 'The Fire Sermon'. This seems to me to be right, for Eliot changed poetry as much as Wordsworth did, in his time, though no great poet is ever working alone, for as the Time-spirit changes, all poets are both active and passive in its change.

Among the poets to whom I am grateful for more suggestions than I could use, are John Greening who pointed out the Owen, and Peter Redgrove's 'Staines Waterworks', as well as several others; Sylvia Bradford who set me hunting through Morris, and Anne Stevenson who told me of John Taylor. He was a seventeenth-century working man who came to be known as the 'Water Poet' because he was a Thames waterman. He rowed people across the river in his boat, taking them from the City to the theatres on the Southwark side, and then back again. In one poem he welcomes a more celebrated versifier into his boat with –

> Sir, lend me your worship's hand.
> Take heed, t'hath rain'd, 'tis slippery, Sir to stand.
> But sit you downe, we have the wind and tide,
> Good Sir, a little on the Star-board side.
> Thrust off now; I am glad I have you here,

Good *Master Fennor (alias) Le Fegnier.*
You are a fare falne to my lot divinely,
Trim you my boat, and I will trim you finely:
And as I Row, Ile tell you who I am;
I am John Taylor made your Annagram.

Then follow insults that, though fairly harmless, cannot but have dis-
couraged his poetic rivals from stepping into his boat a second time.
He was clearly a very lively man. He wrote a pamphlet against the
building of theatres on the north side of the Thames, so that the
ferry-boats to the south bank theatres became unnecessary, and
watermen lost their livings; and another against the proliferation of
road traffic, called *The World runs on Wheeles*. He practically invented
the sponsored walk, and went on foot to Edinburgh on the strength
of 1,600 signatures, and published *The Pennyless Pilgrimage* on his
return. This sold 4,500 copies, and was a best-seller in its day.

No doubt another, and fatter, Thames anthology should be made,
and Taylor's life and works deserve a book to themselves. And they
have one, for my information comes from a facsimile, produced by
the Scolar Press in 1973, of the complete works of John Taylor, as
published in 1630.

Major rivers usually end with an estuary, so Ruth Pitter's poem is
placed at the end of this Thames, although she was of the generation
that was nearly twenty years old in 1914, in time for the Great War,
but, unlike so many, she lived to be nearly 100, and died quite
recently. But I must end by mentioning Rudyard Kipling, whose
vigorous prehistoric history, in couplets packed with familiar place-
names, so that past and present become one, originally gave me the
idea for this book.

ANNA ADAMS
Chiswick, February 1999

RUDYARD KIPLING
(1865-1936)

The River's Tale
(PREHISTORIC)

> *Twenty bridges from Tower to Kew –*
> *(Twenty bridges or twenty-two) –*
> *Wanted to know what the River knew,*
> *For they were young and the Thames was old.*
> *And this is the tale that the River told: –*

'I walk my beat before London Town,
Five hours up and seven down.
Up I go till I end my run
At Tide-end-town, which is Teddington.
Down I come with the mud in my hands
And plaster it over the Maplin Sands.
But I'd have you know that these waters of mine
Were once a branch of the River Rhine,
When hundreds of miles to the East I went
And England was joined to the Continent.

I remember the bat-winged lizard-birds,
The Age of Ice and the mammoth herds,
And the giant tigers that stalked them down
Through Regent's Park into Camden Town.
And I remember like yesterday
The earliest Cockney who came my way,
When he pushed through the forest that lined the Strand
With paint on his face and a club in his hand.
He was death to feather and fin and fur.
He trapped my beavers at Westminster.
He netted my salmon, he hunted my deer,
He killed my heron off Lambeth Pier.
He fought his neighbour with axes and swords,
Flint or bronze, at my upper fords,
While down at Greenwich, for slaves and tin,
The tall Phoenician ships stole in,
And North Sea war-boats, painted and gay,

Flashed like dragon-flies, Erith way;
And Norseman and Negro and Gaul and Greek
Drank with the Britons in Barking Creek,
And life was gay, and the world was new,
And I was a mile across at Kew!
But the Roman came with a heavy hand,
And bridged and roaded and ruled the land,
And the Roman left and the Danes blew in –
And that's where your history-books begin!'

WILLIAM DUNBAR
(c.1460–c.1520)

In Honour of the City of London

London, thou art of townes *A per se*.
   Soveraign of cities, seemliest in sight,
Of high renoun, riches and royaltie;
   Of lordis, barons, and many a goodly knyght;
   Of most delectable lusty ladies bright;
Of famous prelatis, in habitis clericall;
   Of merchauntis full of substaunce and of myght:
London, thou art the flour of Cities all.

Gladdith[1] anon, thou lusty Troynovaunt,[2]
   Citie that some tyme cleped was New Troy;
In all the erth, imperiall as thou stant,
   Pryncesse of townes, of pleasure and of joy,
   A richer restith under no Christen roy;
For manly power, with craftis naturall,
   Fourmeth none fairer sith[3] the flode of Noy:
London, thou art the flour of Cities all.

Gemme of all joy, jasper of jocunditie,
   Most myghty carbuncle of vertue and valour;
Strong Troy in vigour and in strenuytie;
   Of royall cities rose and geraflour;[4]
   Empress of townes, exalt in honour;
In beawtie beryng the crone imperiall;
   Swete paradise precelling in pleasure;
London, thou art the flour of Cities all.

Above all ryvers thy Ryver hath renowne,
   Whose beryall stremys, pleasaunt and preclare
Under thy lusty wallys renneth down,
   Where many a swan doth swymme with wyngis fair;

---

[1] rejoice.   [2] Troja nova or Trinovantum.   [3] since.   [4] gillyflower.

Where many a barge doth saile and row with are;[1]
Where many a ship doth rest with top-royall.
O, towne of townes! patrone and not compare,[2]
London, thou art the flour of Cities all.

Upon thy lusty Brigge of pylers white
   Been merchauntis full royall to behold;
Upon thy stretis goeth many a semely knyght
   In velvet gownes and in cheynes of gold.
   By Julyus Cesar thy Tour founded of old
May be the hous of Mars victoryall,
   Whose artillary with tonge may not be told:
London, thou art the flour of Cities all.

Strong by thy wallis that about thee standis;
   Wise be the people that within thee dwellis;
Fresh is thy ryver with his lusty strandis;
   Blith be thy chirches, wele sownyng be thy bellis;
   Rich be thy merchauntis in substaunce that excellis;
Fair be their wives, right lovesom, white and small,[3]
   Clere by thy virgyns, lusty under kellis:[4]
London, thou art the flour of Cities all.

Thy famous Maire, by pryncely governaunce,
   With sword of justice thee ruleth prudently.
No Lord of Parys, Venyce, or Flouraunce
   In dignitye or honour goeth to hym nigh.
   He is exampler, loode-ster, and guye;
Principall patrone and rose orygynalle,
   Above all Maires as maister most worthy:
London, thou art the flour of Cities all.

---

[1] oar.   [2] compeer.   [3] slender.   [4] hoods, head-dresses.

EDMUND SPENSER
(c.1552-99)

Prothalamion

Calm was the day, and through the trembling air
Sweet-breathing Zephyrus did softly play –
A gentle spirit, that lightly did delay
Hot Titan's beams, which then did glister fair;
When I, (whom sullen care,
Through discontent of my long fruitless stay
In princes' court, and expectation vain
Of idle hopes, which still do fly away
Like empty shadows, did afflict my brain)
Walk'd forth to ease my pain
Along the shore of silver-streaming Thames;
Whose rutty bank, the which his river hems,
Was painted all with variable flowers,
And all the meads adorn'd with dainty gems
Fit to deck maidens' bowers,
And crown their paramours
Against the bridal day, which is not long:
    Sweet Thames! run softly, till I end my song.

There in a meadow by the river's side
A flock of nymphs I chancéd to espy,
All lovely daughters of the flood thereby,
With goodly greenish locks all loose untied
As each had been a bride;
And each one had a little wicker basket
Made of fine twigs, entrailéd curiously,
In which they gather'd flowers to fill their flasket,
And with fine fingers cropt full feateously
The tender stalks on high.
Of every sort which in that meadow grew
They gather'd some; the violet, pallid blue,
The little daisy that at evening closes,
The virgin lily and the primrose true:
With store of vermeil roses,
To deck their bridegrooms' posies

Against the bridal day, which was not long:
Sweet Thames! run softly, till I end my song.

With that I saw two swans of goodly hue
Come softly swimming down along the Lee;
Two fairer birds I yet did never see;
The snow which doth the top of Pindus strow
Did never whiter show,
Nor Jove himself, when he a swan would be
For love of Leda, whiter did appear;
Yet Leda was (they say) as white as he,
Yet not so white as these, nor nothing near;
So purely white they were
That even the gentle stream, the which them bare,
Seem'd foul to them, and bade his billows spare
To wet their silken feathers, lest they might
Soil their fair plumes with water not so fair,
And mar their beauties bright
That shone as Heaven's light
Against their bridal day, which was not long:
Sweet Thames! run softly, till I end my song.

Eftsoons the nymphs, which now had flowers their fill,
Ran all in haste to see that silver brood
As they came floating on the crystal flood;
Whom when they saw, they stood amazéd still
Their wondering eyes to fill;
Them seem'd they never saw a sight so fair
Of fowls, so lovely, that they sure did deem
Them heavenly born, or to be that same pair
Which through the sky draw Venus' silver team;
For sure they did not seem
To be begot of any earthly seed,
But rather angels, or of angels' breed;
Yet were they bred of summer's heat, they say,
In sweetest season, when each flower and weed
The earth did fresh array;
So fresh they seem'd as day,
Ev'n as their bridal day, which was not long:
Sweet Thames! run softly, till I end my song.

Then forth they all out of their baskets drew
Great store of flowers, the honour of the field,
That to the sense did fragrant odours yield,
All which upon those goodly birds they threw
And all the waves did strew,
That like old Peneus' waters they did seem
When down along by pleasant Tempe's shore
Scatter'd with flowers, through Thessaly they stream,
That they appear, through lilies' plenteous store,
Like a bride's chamber-floor.
Two of those nymphs meanwhile two garlands bound
Of freshest flowers which in that mead they found,
The which presenting all in trim array,
Their snowy foreheads therewithal they crown'd;
Whilst one did sing this lay
Prepared against that day,
Against their bridal day, which was not long:
   Sweet Thames! run softly, till I end my song.

'Ye gentle birds! the world's fair ornament,
And Heaven's glory, whom this happy hour
Doth lead unto your lovers' blissful bower,
Joy may you have, and gentle heart's content
Of your love's couplement;
And let fair Venus, that is queen of love,
With her heart-quelling son upon you smile,
Whose smile, they say, hath virtue to remove
All love's dislike, and friendship's faulty guile
For ever to assoil.
Let endless peace your steadfast hearts accord,
And blessèd plenty wait upon your board;
And let your bed with pleasures chaste abound,
That fruitful issue may to you afford
Which may your foes confound,
And make your joys redound
Upon your bridal day, which is not long:
   Sweet Thames! run softly, till I end my song.'

So ended she; and all the rest around
To her redoubled that her undersong,
Which said their bridal day should not be long:

And gentle Echo from the neighbour ground
Their accents did resound.
So forth those joyous birds did pass along
Adown the Lee that to them murmur'd low,
As he would speak but that he lack'd a tongue;
Yet did by signs his glad affection show,
Making his stream run slow.
And all the fowl which in his flood did dwell
'Gan flock about these twain, that did excel
The rest, so far as Cynthia doth shend
The lesser stars. So they, enrangéd well,
Did on those two attend,
And their best service lend
Against their wedding day, which was not long:
    Sweet Thames! run softly, till I end my song.

At length they all to merry London came,
To merry London, my most kindly nurse,
That to me gave this life's first native source,
Though from another place I take my name,
An house of ancient fame:
There when they came whereas those bricky towers
The which on Thames' broad aged back do ride,
Where now the studious lawyers have their bowers,
Their whilome wont the Templar-knights to bide,
Till they decay'd through pride;
Next whereunto there stands a stately place,
Where oft I gainéd gifts and goodly grace
Of that great lord, which therein wont to dwell,
Whose want too well now feels my friendless case;
But ah! here fits not well
Old woes, but joys to tell
Against the bridal day, which is not long:
    Sweet Thames! run softly, till I end my song.

Yet therein now doth lodge a noble peer,
Great England's glory and the world's wide wonder,
Whose dreadful name late through all Spain did thunder,
And Hercules' two pillars standing near
Did make to quake and fear:
Fair branch of honour, flower of chivalry!

That fillest England with thy triumphs' fame
Joy have thou of thy noble victory,
And endless happiness of thine own name
That promiseth the same;
That through thy prowess and victorious arms
Thy country may be freed from foreign harms,
And great Elisa's glorious name may ring
Through all the world, fill'd with thy wide alarms,
Which some brave Muse may sing
To ages following:
Upon the bridal day, which is not long:
  Sweet Thames! run softly, till I end my song.

From those high towers this noble lord issúing
Like radiant Hesper, when his golden hair
In th' ocean billows he hath bathéd fair,
Descended to the river's open viewing
With a great train ensuing.
Above the rest were goodly to be seen
Two gentle knights of lovely face and feature,
Beseeming well the bower of any queen,
With gifts of wit and ornaments of nature,
Fit for so goodly stature,
That like the twins of Jove they seem'd in sight
Which deck the baldric of the Heavens bright;
They two, forth pacing to the river's side,
Received those two fair brides, their love's delight;
Which, at th' appointed tide,
Each one did make his bride
Against their bridal day, which is not long:
  Sweet Thames! run softly, till I end my song.

SIR JOHN DENHAM
(1615-69)

The Thames from Cooper's Hill

My eye descending from the hill surveys
Where Thames amongst the wanton valleys strays.
Thames, the most lov'd of all the Ocean's sons,
By his old sire to his embraces runs,
Hasting to pay his tribute to the sea,
Like mortal life to meet eternity.
Though with those streams he no resemblance hold,
Whose foam is amber, and their gravel gold,
His genuine, and less guilty, wealth t'explore,
Search not his bottom, but survey his shore;
O'er which he kindly spreads his spacious wing,
And hatches plenty for th'ensuing spring.
Nor then destroys it with too fond a stay
Like mothers who their infants overlay.
Nor with a sudden and impetuous wave,
Like profuse kings, resumes the wealth he gave.
No unexpected inundations spoil
The mower's hopes, nor mock the ploughman's toil:
But god-like his unwearied bounty flows,
First loves to do, then loves the good he does.
Nor are his blessings to his banks confin'd,
But free and common, as the sea or wind;
When he to boast, or to disperse his stores
Full of the tributes of his grateful shores,
Visits the world, and in his flying towers
Brings home to us, and makes both Indies ours;
Finds wealth where 'tis, bestows it where it wants,
Cities in deserts, woods in cities plants.
So that to us no thing, no place, is strange,
While his fair bosom is the world's exchange.
O could I flow like thee, and make thy stream
My great example, as it is my theme!
Though deep, yet clear, though gentle, yet not dull,
Strong without rage, without o'erflowing full.

JOHN DRYDEN
(1631–1700)

London After the Great Fire, 1666

Methinks already from this chymic flame
I see a city of more precious mould,
Rich as the town which gives the Indies name,
With silver paved and all divine with gold.

Already, labouring with a mighty fate,
She shakes the rubbish from her mounting brow,
And seems to have renewed her charter's date,
Which Heaven will to the death of time allow.

More great than human now and more August,
New deified she from her fires does rise:
Her widening streets on new foundations trust,
And, opening, into larger parts she flies.

Before, she like some shepherdess did show
Who sat to bathe her by a river's side,
Not answering to her fame, but rude and low,
Nor taught the beauteous arts of modern pride.

Now like a maiden queen she will behold
From her high turrets hourly suitors come;
The East with incense and the West with gold
Will stand like suppliants to receive her doom.

The silver Thames, her own domestic flood,
Shall bear her vessels like a sweeping train,
And often wind, as of his mistress proud,
With longing eyes to meet her face again.

The wealthy Tagus and the wealthier Rhine
The glory of their towns no more shall boast,
And Seine, that would with Belgian rivers join,
Shall find her lustre stained and traffic lost.

The venturous merchant who designed more far
And touches on our hospitable shore,
Charmed with the splendour of this northern star,
Shall here unlade him and depart no more.

ALEXANDER POPE
(1688-1744)

The Voyage on the Thames
from *The Rape of the Lock*

Not with more glories, in the etherial plain,
The Sun first rises o'er the purpled main,
Than, issuing forth, the rival of his beams
Launched on the bosom of the silver Thames.
Fair nymphs and well-dressed youths around her shone,
But every eye was fixed on her alone.
On her white breast a sparkling cross she wore,
Which Jews might kiss, and Infidels adore.
Her lively looks a sprightly mind disclose,
Quick as her eyes, and as unfixed as those:
Favours to none, to all she smiles extends;
Oft she rejects, but never once offends.

. . . .

But now secure the painted vessel glides,
The sun-beams trembling on the floating tides;
While melting music steals upon the sky,
And softened sounds along the waters die;
Smooth flow the waves, the Zephyrs gently play,
Belinda smiled, and all the world was gay.
All but the Sylph – with careful thoughts oppressed,
The impending woe sat heavy on his breast.
He summons straight his denizens of air;
The lucid squadrons round the sails repair:
Soft o'er the shrouds aerial whispers breathe,
That seemed but Zephyrs to the train beneath.
Some to the sun their insect-wings unfold,
Waft on the breeze, or sink in clouds of gold;
Transparent forms, too fine for mortal sight,
Their fluid bodies half dissolved in light.
Loose to the winds their airy garments flew,
Thin glittering textures of the filmy dew,

25

Dipped in the richest tincture of the skies,
Where light disports in ever-mingling dyes,
While every beam new transient colours flings,
Colours that change when'er they wave their wings.

THOMAS GRAY
(1716-71)

Ode on a Distant Prospect of Eton College

Ye distant spires, ye antique towers,
That crown the watry glade,
Where grateful Science still adores
Her Henry's* holy Shade;
And ye, that from the stately brow
Of Windsor's heights th' expanse below
Of grove, of lawn, of mead survey,
Whose turf, whose shade, whose flowers among
Wanders the hoary Thames along
His silver-winding way.

Ah happy hills, ah pleasing shade,
Ah fields belov'd in vain,
Where once my careless childhood stray'd,
A stranger yet to pain!
I feel the gales, that from ye blow,
A momentary bliss bestow,
As waving fresh their gladsome wing,
My weary soul they seem to sooth,
And, redolent of joy and youth,
To breathe a second spring.

Say, Father Thames, for thou hast seen
Full many a sprightly race
Disporting on thy margent green
The paths of pleasure trace,
Who foremost now delight to cleave
With pliant arm thy glassy wave?
The captive linnet which enthrall?
What idle progeny succeed
To chase the rolling circle's speed,
Or urge the flying ball?

---

* King Henry the Sixth, Founder of the College.

While some on earnest business bent
Their murm'ring labours ply
'Gainst graver hours, that bring constraint
To sweeten liberty:
Some bold adventurers disdain
The limits of their little reign,
And unknown regions dare descry:
Still as they run they look behind,
They hear a voice in every wind,
And snatch a fearful joy.

Gay hope is theirs by fancy fed,
Less pleasing when possest;
The tear forgot as soon as shed,
The sunshine of the breast:
Theirs buxom health of rosy hue,
Wild wit, invention ever-new,
And lively chear of vigour born;
The thoughtless day, the easy night,
The spirits pure, the slumbers light,
That fly th' approach of morn.

Alas, regardless of their doom,
The little victims play!
No sense have they of ills to come,
Nor care beyond to-day:
Yet see how all around 'em wait
The Ministers of human fate,
And black Misfortune's baleful train!
Ah, shew them where in ambush stand
To seize their prey the murth'rous band!
Ah, tell them, they are men!

These shall the fury Passions tear,
The vulturs of the mind,
Disdainful Anger, pallid Fear,
And Shame that sculks behind;
Or pineing Love shall waste their youth,
Or Jealousy with rankling tooth,
That inly gnaws the secret heart,
And Envy wan, and faded Care,

Grim-visag'd comfortless Despair,
And Sorrow's piercing dart.

    Ambition this shall tempt to rise,
Then whirl the wretch from high,
To bitter Scorn a sacrifice,
And grinning Infamy.
The stings of Falsehood those shall try,
And hard Unkindness' alter'd eye,
That mocks the tear it forc'd to flow;
And keen Remorse with blood defil'd,
And moody Madness laughing wild
Amid severest woe.

    Lo, in the vale of years beneath
A griesly troop are seen,
The painful family of Death,
More hideous than their Queen:
This racks the joints, this fires the veins,
That every labouring sinew strains,
Those in the deeper vitals rage:
Lo, Poverty, to fill the band,
That numbs the soul with icy hand,
And slow-consuming Age.

    To each his suff'rings: all are men,
Condemn'd alike to groan,
The tender for another's pain;
Th' unfeeling for his own.
Yet ah! why should they know their fate?
Since sorrow never comes too late,
And happiness too swiftly flies.
Thought would destroy their paradise.
No more; where ignorance is bliss,
'Tis folly to be wise.

WILLIAM BLAKE
(1757-1827)

London

I wander thro' each charter'd street,
Near where the charter'd Thames does flow,
And mark in every face I meet
Marks of weakness, marks of woe.

In every cry of every Man,
In every infant's cry of fear,
In every voice, in every ban,
The mind-forg'd manacles I hear.

How the Chimney-sweeper's cry
Every black'ning Church appals;
And the hapless Soldier's sigh
Runs in blood down Palace walls.

But most thro' midnight streets I hear
How the youthful Harlot's curse
Blasts the new born Infant's tear,
And blights with plagues the Marriage hearse.

WILLIAM BLAKE
(1757-1827)

Why should I care for the men of Thames,
Or the cheating waves of charter'd streams,
Or shrink at the little blasts of fear
That the hireling blows into my ear?

Tho' born on the cheating banks of Thames,
Tho' his waters bathed my infant limbs,
The Ohio shall wash his stains from me:
I was born a slave, but I go to be free.

WILLIAM WORDSWORTH
(1770–1850)

Upon Westminster Bridge
Sept. 3, 1802

Earth has not anything to show more fair:
　　Dull would he be of soul who could pass by
　　A sight so touching in its majesty:
This City now doth, like a garment, wear
The beauty of the morning; silent, bare,
　　Ships, towers, domes, theatres, and temples lie
　　Open unto the fields, and to the sky;
All bright and glittering in the smokeless air.
Never did sun more beautifully steep
　　In his first splendour, valley, rock, or hill;
Ne'er saw I, never felt, a calm so deep!
　　The river glideth at his own sweet will:
Dear God! the very houses seem asleep;
　　And all that mighty heart is lying still!

THOMAS HARDY
(1840-1928)

A Wife in London
(December 1899)

I

She sits in the tawny vapour
    That the Thames-side lanes have uprolled,
    Behind whose webby fold on fold
Like a waning taper
    The street-lamp glimmers cold.

A messenger's knock cracks smartly,
    Flashed news is in her hand
    Of meaning it dazes to understand
Though shaped so shortly:
    He – has fallen – in the far South Land. . . .

II

'Tis the morrow; the fog hangs thicker,
    The postman nears and goes:
    A letter is brought whose lines disclose
By the firelight flicker
    His hand, whom the worm now knows:

Fresh – firm – penned in highest feather –
    Page-full of his hoped return,
    And of home-planned jaunts by brake and burn
In the summer weather,
    And of new love that they would learn.

ALICE MEYNELL
(1847–1922)

The Visiting Sea

As the inhastening tide doth roll,
Home from the deep, along the whole
   Wide shining strand, and floods the caves,
   – Your love comes filling with happy waves
The open sea-shore of my soul.

But inland from the seaward spaces,
None knows, not even you, the places
   Brimmed, at your coming, out of sight,
   – The little solitudes of delight
This tide constrains in dim embraces.

You see the happy shore, wave-rimmed,
But know not of the quiet dimmed
   Rivers your coming floods and fills,
   The little pools 'mid happier hills,
My silent rivulets, over-brimmed.

What! I have secrets from you? Yes.
But, visiting Sea, your love doth press
   And reach in further than you know,
   And fills all these; and, when you go,
There's loneliness in loneliness.

FRANCIS THOMPSON
(1859-1907)

In No Strange Land

O world invisible, we view thee,
O world intangible, we touch thee,
O world unknowable, we know thee,
Inapprehensible, we clutch thee!

Does the fish soar to find the ocean,
The eagle plunge to find the air —
That we ask of the stars in motion
If they have rumour of thee there?

Not where the wheeling systems darken,
And our benumbed conceiving soars! —
The drift of pinions, would we hearken,
Beats at our own clay-shuttered doors.

The angels keep their ancient places; —
Turn but a stone, and start a wing!
'Tis ye, 'tis your estrangèd faces,
That miss the many-splendoured thing.

But (when so sad thou canst not sadder)
Cry; — and upon thy so sore loss
Shall shine the traffic of Jacob's ladder
Pitched betwixt Heaven and Charing Cross.

Yes, in the night, my Soul, my daughter,
Cry, — clinging Heaven by the hems;
And lo, Christ walking on the water,
Not of Gennesareth, but Thames!

OSCAR WILDE
(1854-1900)

Symphony in Yellow

An omnibus across the bridge
  Crawls like a yellow butterfly,
    And, here and there, a passer-by
Shows like a little restless midge.

Big barges full of yellow hay
  Are moved against the shadowy wharf,
    And, like a yellow silken scarf,
The thick fog hangs along the quay.

The yellow leaves begin to fade
  And flutter from the Temple elms,
    And at my feet the pale green Thames
Lies like a rod of rippled jade.

CHARLES HAMILTON SORLEY
(1895-1915)

The River

He watched the river running black
   Beneath the blacker sky;
It did not pause upon its track
   Of silent instancy;
It did not hasten, nor was slack,
   But still went gliding by.

It was so black. There was no wind
   Its patience to defy.
It was not that the man had sinned,
   Or that he wished to die.
Only the wide and silent tide
   Went slowly sweeping by.

The mass of blackness moving down
   Filled full of dreams the eye;
The lights of all the lighted town
   Upon its breast did lie;
The tall black trees were upside down
   In the river phantasy.

He had an envy for its black
   Inscrutability;
He felt impatiently the lack
   Of that great law whereby
The river never travels back
   But still goes gliding by;

But still goes gliding by, nor clings
   To passing things that die,
Nor shows the secrets that it brings
   From its strange source on high.
And he felt 'We are two living things
   And the weaker one is I.'

He saw the town, that living stack
   Piled up against the sky.
He saw the river running black
   On, on and on: O, why
Could he not move along his track
   With such consistency?

He had a yearning for the strength
   That comes of unity:
The union of one soul at length
   With its twin-soul to lie:
To be a part of one great strength
   That moves and cannot die.

*   *   *   *   *   *

He watched the river running black
   Beneath the blacker sky.
He pulled his coat about his back,
   He did not strive nor cry.
He put his foot upon the track
   That still went gliding by.

The thing that never travels back
   Received him silently.
And there was left no shred, no wrack
   To show the reason why:
Only the river running black
   Beneath the blacker sky.

WILFRED OWEN
(1893-1918)

Shadwell Stair

I am the ghost of Shadwell Stair.
    Along the wharves by the water-house,
    And through the dripping slaughter-house,
I am the shadow that walks there.

Yet I have flesh both firm and cool,
    And eyes tumultuous as the gems
    Of moons and lamps in the lapping Thames
When dusk sails wavering down the pool.

Shuddering the purple street-arc burns
    Where I watch always; from the banks
    Dolorously the shipping clanks,
And after me a strange tide turns.

I walk till the stars of London wane
    And dawn creeps up the Shadwell Stair.
    But when the crowing syrens blare
I with another ghost am lain.

T. S. ELIOT
(1888-1965)

The Fire Sermon
from *The Waste Land*

   The river's tent is broken; the last fingers of leaf
Clutch and sink into the wet bank. The wind
Crosses the brown land, unheard. The nymphs are departed.
Sweet Thames, run softly, till I end my song.
The river bears no empty bottles, sandwich papers,
Silk handkerchiefs, cardboard boxes, cigarette ends
Or other testimony of summer nights. The nymphs are departed.
And their friends, the loitering heirs of City directors;
Departed, have left no addresses.
By the waters of Leman I sat down and wept . . .
Sweet Thames, run softly till I end my song,
Sweet Thames, run softly, for I speak not loud or long.
But at my back in a cold blast I hear
The rattle of the bones, and chuckle spread from ear to ear.

A rat crept softly through the vegetation
Dragging its slimy belly on the bank
While I was fishing in the dull canal
On a winter evening round behind the gashouse
Musing upon the king my brother's wreck
And on the king my father's death before him.
White bodies naked on the low damp ground
And bones cast in a little low dry garret,
Rattled by the rat's foot only, year to year.
But at my back from time to time I hear
The sound of horns and motors, which shall bring
Sweeney to Mrs. Porter in the spring.

O the moon shone bright on Mrs. Porter
And on her daughter
They wash their feet in soda water
Et O ces voix d'enfants, chantant dans la coupole!

Twit twit twit
Jug jug jug jug jug jug
So rudely forc'd.
Tereu

Unreal City
Under the brown fog of a winter noon
Mr. Eugenides, the Smyrna merchant
Unshaven, with a pocket full of currants
C.i.f. London: documents at sight,
Asked me in demotic French
To luncheon at the Cannon Street Hotel
Followed by a weekend at the Metropole.

At the violet hour, when the eyes and back
Turn upward from the desk, when the human engine waits
Like a taxi throbbing waiting,
I Tiresias, though blind, throbbing between two lives,
Old man with wrinkled female breasts, can see
At the violet hour, the evening hour that strives
Homeward, and brings the sailor home from sea,
The typist home at teatime, clears her breakfast, lights
Her stove, and lays out food in tins.
Out of the window perilously spread
Her drying combinations touched by the sun's last rays,
On the divan are piled (at night her bed)
Stockings, slippers, camisoles, and stays.
I Tiresias, old man with wrinkled dugs
Perceived the scene, and foretold the rest –
I too awaited the expected guest.
He, the young man carbuncular, arrives,
A small house agent's clerk, with one bold stare,
One of the low on whom assurance sits
As a silk hat on a Bradford millionaire.
The time is now propitious, as he guesses,
The meal is ended, she is bored and tired,
Endeavours to engage her in caresses
Which still are unreproved, if undesired.
Flushed and decided, he assaults at once;
Exploring hands encounter no defence;
His vanity requires no response,

41

And makes a welcome of indifference.
(And I Tiresias have foresuffered all
Enacted on this same divan or bed;
I who have sat by Thebes below the wall
And walked among the lowest of the dead.)
Bestows one final patronising kiss,
And gropes his way, finding the stairs unlit . . .

    She turns and looks a moment in the glass,
Hardly aware of her departed lover;
Her brain allows one half-formed thought to pass:
'Well now that's done: and I'm glad it's over.'
When lovely woman stoops to folly and
Paces about her room again, alone,
She smooths her hair with automatic hand,
And puts a record on the gramophone.

    'This music crept by me upon the waters'
And along the Strand, up Queen Victoria Street.
O City city, I can sometimes hear
Beside a public bar in Lower Thames Street,
The pleasant whining of a mandoline
And a clatter and a chatter from within
Where fishermen lounge at noon: where the walls
Of Magnus Martyr hold
Inexplicable splendour of Ionian white and gold.

> The river sweats
> Oil and tar
> The barges drift
> With the turning tide
> Red sails
> Wide
> To leeward, swing on the heavy spar.
> The barges wash
> Drifting logs
> Down Greenwich reach
> Past the Isle of Dogs.
> > Weialala leia
> > Wallala leialala

Elizabeth and Leicester
Beating oars
The stern was formed
A gilded shell
Red and gold
The brisk swell
Rippled both shores
Southwest wind
Carried down stream
The peal of bells
White towers
        Weialala leia
        Wallala leialala

'Trams and dusty trees.
Highbury bore me. Richmond and Kew
Undid me. By Richmond I raised my knees
Supine on the floor of a narrow canoe.'

'My feet are at Moorgate, and my heart
Under my feet. After the event
He wept. He promised "a new start."
I made no comment. What should I resent?'

'On Margate Sands.
I can connect
Nothing with nothing.
The broken fingernails of dirty hands.
My people humble people who expect
Nothing.'
        la la

To Carthage then I came

Burning burning burning burning
O Lord Thou pluckest me out
O Lord Thou pluckest

burning

43

DAVID GASCOYNE
(b. 1916)

Extract from *Megalometropolitan Carnival*
from *Night Thoughts*

[Voice C]
At night I've often walked on the Embankment of the Thames
And seen the Power Station's brick cliffs dominate the scene
Over on the South Bank, and its twin pairs of giant stacks
Outpouring over London their perpetual offering
Of smoke in heavy swags fit for a sacrificial rite
Propitiating some brute Carthaginian deity;
And thought they stood like symbols for the worship of our age:
The pillars of a temple raised to man-made Power and Light.

GEORGE BARKER
(1913-91)

Battersea Park
To Anne Ridler

Now it is November and mist wreathes the trees,
The horses cough their white blooms in the street,
Dogs shiver and boys run; the barges on the Thames
Lie like leviathans in the fog; and I meet
A world of lost wonders as I loiter in the haze
Where fog and sorrow cross my April days.

I recollect it was so often thus; with
Diamonds and pearls like mineral water pointing
The Park railings and the gardens' evergreens:
I spent my winters in summer's disappointments.
The things that burned so bright in my Augusts
Scattering me with their November dusts.

Now I marvel that I am again investigating
The fringes of the bare gardens in the winter.
I had expected to be otherwhere now,
Where the worm coils about the bone's splinter.
Now what good is the great world where I walk
That only revives desire to live once more?

How in the fog of failure and distress
Glitter of things seen in a flicker can
Paralyse will and deter determination,
Make a man afraid of the ghost of a man.
It is the wile of the world of crystal things
That catch the eye and keep me in their rings.

What I saw was Sorrow loitering along by
The Thames near the tall bridge by Battersea Park;
He had in his hand Pavlova or a swan,
And I heard him singing softly in the dark:
My twin, he sang to me, whatever of thine
Is sad and sorry, shall be glad of mine.

And he went on, singing a gay tune.
And now I know that the sorrow is this,
Not that the world a space of sorrow is
But that it's glad. O so gay a grief!
How can I ever be at home here
Where Sorrow sings of Joy in my ears?

How can I ever be happy here, where
Cock robin whistles with a gun at his breast;
Here where the flower has for bud a tear,
Here where Beauty breeds fodder for the Beast?
How can I here be happy, when I know
I can be happy only here and now?

DYLAN THOMAS
(1914-53)

A Refusal to Mourn the Death,
by Fire, of a Child in London

Never until the mankind making
Bird beast and flower
Fathering and all humbling darkness
Tells with silence the last light breaking
And the still hour
Is come of the sea tumbling in harness

And I must enter again the round
Zion of the water bead
And the synagogue of the ear of corn
Shall I let pray the shadow of a sound
Or sow my salt seed
In the least valley of sackcloth to mourn

The majesty and burning of the child's death.
I shall not murder
The mankind of her going with a grave truth
Nor blaspheme down the stations of the breath
With any further
Elegy of innocence and youth.

Deep with the first dead lies London's daughter,
Robed in the long friends,
The grains beyond age, the dark veins of her mother,
Secret by the unmourning water
Of the riding Thames.
After the first death, there is no other.

LOUIS MACNEICE
(1907–63)

Charon

The conductor's hands were black with money:
Hold on to your ticket, he said, the inspector's
Mind is black with suspicion, and hold on to
That dissolving map. We moved through London,
We could see the pigeons through the glass but failed
To hear their rumours of wars, we could see
The lost dog barking but never knew
That his bark was as shrill as a cock crowing,
We just jogged on, at each request
Stop there was a crowd of aggressively vacant
Faces, we just jogged on, eternity
Gave itself airs in revolving lights
And then we came to the Thames and all
The bridges were down, the further shore
Was lost in fog, so we asked the conductor
What we should do. He said: Take the ferry
Faute de mieux. We flicked the flashlight
And there was the ferryman just as Virgil
And Dante had seen him. He looked at us coldly
And his eyes were dead and his hands on the oar
Were black with obols and varicose veins
Marbled his calves and he said to us coldly:
If you want to die you will have to pay for it.

STEVIE SMITH
(1902-71)

The River God

I may be smelly and I may be old,
Rough in my pebbles, reedy in my pools,
But where my fish float by I bless their swimming
And I like the people to bathe in me, especially women.
But I can drown the fools
Who bathe too close to the weir, contrary to rules.
And they take a long time drowning
As I throw them up now and then in a spirit of clowning.
Hi yih, yippity-yap, merrily I flow,
O I may be an old foul river but I have plenty of go.
Once there was a lady who was too bold
She bathed in me by the tall black cliff where the water runs cold,
So I brought her down here
To be my beautiful dear.
Oh will she stay with me will she stay
This beautiful lady, or will she go away?
She lies in my beautiful deep river bed with many a weed
To hold her, and many a waving reed.
Oh who would guess what a beautiful white face lies there
Waiting for me to smooth and wash away the fear
She looks at me with. Hi yih, do not let her
Go. There is no one on earth who does not forget her
Now. They say I am a foolish old smelly river
But they do not know of my wide original bed
Where the lady waits, with her golden sleepy head.
If she wishes to go I will not forgive her.

U. A. FANTHORPE
(b. 1929)

Rising Damp

(for C. A. K. and R. K. M.)

'A river can sometimes be diverted, but it is a very hard thing to
lose it altogether.'
                    J. G. Head, paper read to the Auctioneers' Institute in 1907

At our feet they lie low,
The little fervent underground
Rivers of London

Effra, Graveney, Falcon, Quaggy,
Wandle, Walbrook, Tyburn, Fleet

Whose names are disfigured,
Frayed, effaced.

These are the Magogs that chewed the clay
To the basin that London nestles in.
These are the currents that chiselled the city,
That washed the clothes and turned the mills,
Where children drank and salmon swam
And wells were holy.

They have gone under.
Boxed, like the magician's assistant.
Buried alive in earth.
Forgotten, like the dead.

They return spectrally after heavy rain,
Confounding suburban gardens. They infiltrate
Chronic bronchitis statistics. A silken
Slur haunts dwellings by shrouded
Watercourses, and is taken
For the footing of the dead.

Being of our world, they will return
(Westbourne, caged at Sloane Square,
Will jack from his box),
Will deluge cellars, detonate manholes,
Plant effluent on our faces,
Sink the city.

Effra, Graveney, Falcon, Quaggy,
Wandle, Walbrook, Tyburn, Fleet

It is the other rivers that lie
Lower, that touch us only in dreams
That never surface. We feel their tug
As a dowser's rod bends to the source below

Phlegethon, Acheron, Lethe, Styx.

DEREK WALCOTT
(b. 1930)

Extract from *Omeros*

He curled up on a bench underneath the Embankment wall.
He saw London gliding with the Thames around its neck
like a barge which an old brown horse draws up a canal

if its yoke is Time. From here he could see the dreck
under the scrolled skirts of statues, the grit in the stone lions'
eyes; he saw under everything an underlying grime

that itched in the balls of rearing horse stallions,
how the stare of somnolent sphinxes closed in time
to the swaying bells of 'cities all the floure'

petalling the spear-railed park where a couple suns
near the angled shade of All-Hallows by the Tower,
as the tinkling Thames drags by in its ankle-irons,

while the ginkgo's leaves flexed their fingers overhead.
He mutters its fluent alphabet, the peaked A of a spire,
the half-vowels of bridges, down to the crumpled Z

of his overcoat draping a bench in midsummer's fire.
He read the inverted names of boats in their element,
he saw the tugs chirring up a devalued empire

as the coins of their wake passed the Houses of Parliament.
But the shadows keep multiplying from the Outer
Provinces, their dialects light as the ginkgo's leaf, their

fingers plucking their saris as wind picks at water,
and the statues raising objections; he sees a wide river
with its landing of pier-stakes flooding Westminster's

flagstones, and traces the wake of dugouts in the frieze
of a bank's running cornice, and whenever the ginkgo stirs
the wash of far navies settles in the bargeman's eyes.

A statue swims upside down, one hand up in response
to a question raised in the House, and applause rises
from the clapping Thames, from benches in the leaves.

And the sunflower sets after all, retracting its irises
with the bargeman's own, then buds on black, iron trees
as a gliding fog hides the empires: London, Rome, Greece.

PETER REDGROVE
(b. 1932)

Staines Waterworks

I

So it leaps from your taps like a fish
In its sixth and last purification
It is given a coiling motion
By the final rainbow-painted engines, which thunder;
The water is pumped free through these steel shells
Which are conched like the sea –
This is its release from the long train of events
Called *The Waterworks at Staines*.

II

Riverwater gross as gravy is filtered from
Its coarse detritus at the intake and piped
To the sedimentation plant like an Egyptian nightmare,
For it is a hall of twenty pyramids upside-down
Balanced on their points each holding two hundred and fifty
Thousand gallons making thus the alchemical sign
For water and the female triangle.

III

This reverberates like all the halls
With its engines like some moon rolling
And thundering underneath its floors, for in
This windowless hall of tides we do not see the moon.
Here the last solids fall into that sharp tip
For these twenty pyramids are decanters
And there are strong lights at their points
And when sufficient shadow has gathered the automata
Buttle their muddy jets like a river-milk
Out of the many teats of the water-sign.

IV
In the fourth stage this more spiritual water
Is forced through anthracite beds and treated with poison gas,
The verdant chlorine which does not kill it.

V
The habitation of water is a castle, it has turrets
And doors high enough for a mounted knight in armour
To rein in, flourishing his banner, sweating his water,
To gallop along this production line of process where
There are dials to be read as though the castle library-
Books were open on reading-stands at many pages –
But these are automata and the almost-empty halls echo
Emptiness as though you walked the water-conch;
There are very few people in attendance,
All are men and seem very austere
And resemble walking crests of water in their white coats,
Hair white and long in honourable service.

VI
Their cool halls are painted blue and green
Which is the colour of the river in former times,
Purer times, in its flowing rooms.

VII
The final test is a tank of rainbow trout,
The whole station depends on it;
If the fish live, the water is good water.

VIII
In its sixth and last purification
It is given a coiling motion
By vivid yellow and conch-shaped red engines,
This gallery like the broad inside of rainbows
Which rejoice in low thunder over the purification of water,

Trumpeting Staines water triumphantly from spinning conches
    to all taps.

ANDREW MOTION
(b. 1952)

Fresh Water
In Memory of Ruth Haddon

I

This is a long time ago. I am visiting my brother, who is living
near Cirencester, and he says let's go and see the source of the Thames.
It's winter. We leave early, before the sun has taken frost off the fields,

and park in a lane. There's a painful hawthorn hedge with a stile.
When we jump down, our boots gibber on the hard ground.
Then we're striding, kicking ice-dust off the grass to look confident –

because really we're not sure if we're allowed to be here.
In fact we're not even sure that this is the right place.
A friend of a friend has told us; it's all as vague as that.

In the centre of the field we find more hawthorn, a single bush,
and water oozing out of a hole in the ground. I tell my brother
I've read about a statue that stands here, or rather lounges here –

a naked, shaggy-haired god tilting an urn with one massive hand.
Where is he? There's only the empty field glittering,
and a few dowager crows picking among the dock-clumps.

Where is Father Thames? My brother thinks he has been vandalised
and dragged off by the fans of other rivers – they smashed the old
    man's urn,
and sprayed his bare chest and legs with the names of rivals:

Trent, Severn, Nene, Humber. There's nothing else to do,
so I paddle through the shallow water surrounding the spring,
treading carefully to keep things in focus,

and stoop over the source as though I find it fascinating.
It is fascinating. A red-brown soft-lipped cleft
with bright green grass right up to the edge,

and the water twisting out like a rope of glass.
It pulses and shivers as it comes, then steadies
into the pool, then roughens again as it drains into the valley.

My brother and I are not twenty yet. We don't know who we are,
or who we want to be. We stare at the spring, at each other,
and back at the spring again, saying nothing.

A pheasant is making its blatant *kok-kok*
from the wood running along the valley floor.
I stamp both feet and disappear in a cloud.

2

One March there's suddenly a day as warm as May, and my friend
uncovers the punt he has bought as a wreck and restored,
cleans her, slides her into the Thames near Lechlade, and sets off

upriver. Will I go with him? No, I can't.
But I'll meet him on the water meadows at the edge of town.
I turn out of the market square, past the church, and down the
        yew-tree walk.

Shelley visited here once – it's called Shelley's Walk –
but he was out of his element. Here everything is earth
and water, not fire and air. The ground is sleepy-haired

after winter, red berries and rain matted into it.
Where the yew-tree walk ends I go blind in the sun for a moment,
then it's all right. There's the river beyond the boggy meadows,

hidden by reed-forests sprouting along its banks. They're dead,
the reeds – a shambles of broken, broad, pale-brown leaves
and snapped bullrush heads. And there's my friend making

his slow curve towards me. The hills rise behind him
in a gradual wave, so that he seems at the centre
of an enormous amphitheatre. He is an emblem of something;

somebody acting something. The punt pole shoots up
wagging its beard of light, falls, and as he moves ahead
he leans forward, red-faced and concentrating.

He's expert but it's slow work. As I get closer I can hear
water pattering against the prow of the punt,
see him twisting the pole as he plucks it out of the gluey river-bed.

I call to him and he stands straight, giving a wobbly wave.
We burst into laughter. He looks like a madman, floating slowly
backwards now that he has stopped poling. I must look

like a madman too, mud-spattered and heavy-footed on the bank,
wondering how I'm going to get on board without falling in.
As I push open the curtain of leaves to find a way,

I see the water for the first time, solid-seeming and mercury-coloured.
Not like a familiar thing at all. Not looking
as though it could take us anywhere we wanted to go.

3

I've lived here for a while, and up to now the river has been
for pleasure. This evening people in diving suits have taken it over.
Everyone else has been shooshed away into Christchurch Meadow

or onto Folly Bridge like me. No one's complaining. The summer
      evening
expands lazily, big purple and gold clouds building over the Cumnor
      hills.
I have often stood here before. Away to the left you can see Oxford

throwing its spires into the air, full of the conceited joy of being itself.
Straight ahead the river runs calmly between boat-houses
before losing patience again, pulling a reed-shawl round its ears,

snapping off willows and holding their scarified heads underwater.
Now there's a small rowing boat, a kind of coracle below me,
and two policemen with their jackets off. The men shield their eyes,

peering, and almost rock overboard, they're so surprised,
when bubbles erupt beside them and a diver bobs up –
just his head, streaming in its black wet-suit. There are shouts –

See anything? – but the diver shrugs, and twirls his murky torchlight
with an invisible hand. Everyone on the bridge stops talking.
We think we are about to be shown the story of the river-bed –

its shopping trolleys and broken boat-parts, its lolling bottles,
its plastic, its dropped keys, its blubbery and bloated corpse.
But nothing happens. The diver taps his mask and disappears,

his fart-trail surging raucously for a moment, then subsiding.
The crowd in Christchurch Meadow starts to break up.
On Folly Bridge people begin talking again, and as someone steps

off the pavement onto the road, a passing grocery van –
irritated by the press of people, and impatient with whatever
brought them together – gives a long wild *paarp* as it revs away.

4

Now the children are old enough to see what there is to see
we take them to Tower Bridge and explain how the road lifts up,
how traitors arrived at Traitor's Gate, how this was a brewery

and that was a warehouse, how the river starts many miles inland
and changes and grows, changes and grows, until it arrives here,
London, where we live, then winds past Canary Wharf

(which they've done in school) and out to sea.
Afterwards we lean on the railings outside a café. It's autumn.
The water is speckled with leaves, and a complicated tangle of junk

bumps against the embankment wall: a hank of bright grass,
a rotten bullrush stem, a fragment of dark polished wood.
One of the children asks if people drown in the river, and I think

of Ruth, who was on the *Marchioness*. After her death, I met
someone who had survived. He had been in the lavatory when the
dredger hit,
and fumbled his way out along a flooded corridor, his shoes

and clothes miraculously slipping off him, so that when he at last
burst into the air he felt that he was a baby again
and knew nothing, was unable to help himself, aghast.

I touch my wife's arm and the children gather round us.
We are the picture of a family on an outing. I love it. I love the river
and the perky tour-boats with their banal chat. I love the snub barges.

I love the whole dazzling cross-hatchery of traffic and currents,
shadows and sun, standing still and moving forward.
The tangle of junk bumps the wall below me again and I look down.

There is Ruth swimming back upstream, her red velvet party dress
flickering round her heels as she twists through the locks
and dreams round the slow curves, slithering on for miles

until she has passed the ponderous diver at Folly Bridge
and the reed-forests at Lechlade, accelerating beneath bridges and
willow branches,
slinking easily among the plastic wrecks and weedy trolleys,

speeding and shrinking and silvering until finally she is sliding uphill
over bright green grass and into the small wet mouth of the earth,
where she vanishes.

LOTTE KRAMER
(b. 1923)

After the Theatre

Brimful with words.
St Paul's blooming down-river,
Hungerford bridge a chain
Across the Thames whose purse
Opens with teeth of lights.

But curled in corners,
In cardboard, in silence,
The smell of L-and-S-shaped
Heaps of the homeless –
In this nursery of pleasure.

Again, at the escalator's base,
Someone sharing the ground
With rats and mice.
A green youth kneels down
To press a coin into that old fist.

PAULINE STAINER
(b. 1941)

Pouring the Sand Mandala into the Thames

I still hear them –
the Buddhist monks
rasping their cones
of coloured sand

the mandala falling
in a fine stream,
the river wearing
its oiled silks.

It forces the flow –
the treachery of images –
the briar that blooms
as if unpremeditated

then bewilders the bone.

JOHN GREENING
(b. 1954)

The Thames

A river that has coiled about me
like desire: I climbed the very
terraces to school each day,
divined its presence, knew
its power; that it was glimpsed
from Green Lines to Windsor
Great Park, and spotted
on Red Rovers to Battersea
funfair; that it ruled Richmond
and Twickenham and smelt out
Brentford, Isleworth, Hounslow:
that it was near home.
                    My father
like me, Thames-born, dug
the prime alluvial soil
and quoted bits of 'Three Men
in a Boat'; and twice, we
took one out for the day
from Sunbury: 'Beau Geste'
the name I unreeled over
into dark eddies, imagining
a pike or rainbow perch
and catching rudd.
                  There were
stories: a constant wash
of quicksands and drownings; of one
who fell from his boat and caught
Green Monkey Disease; of one
who left his clothes folded
neatly on the bank; of fish
vanishing and fish returning;
of a dolphin at Tower Bridge;
of the coming barrage; of a small
god or a jewelled sword-hilt
salvaged; of a child my age

dragged clear.
My youth
walks the tow-path, looking
up at a tall chimney, grand
Palladian villas, shapely
bridges, feeding the swans
that Spenser knew, unknowing
how rich the fare, but towed
by a Friday grandfather
from his Defoe Avenue home:
a castaway I, aware that
the river could rise and flood
childhood coral as it had in
those sepia photographs – fear
of wet sandbags mingling
with Grandpa's home-grown
tobacco hung up to dry
like seaweed in the chequered
sea-cave of his kitchen, an old
black magnet on his shelf,
an iron Mae West that so
attracts me I clutch at it
and he shouts to me 'Don't –'
through the gas-fire roar
of surf on rocks.
At Kew,
everything started opening:
gardens that seemed the river's
child, the heart of desire,
Eden where I hyperventilate
still under oxygenating glass,
palm, alpine, monkey puzzle,
sacrarium of conkers, open
prospects and a shut pagoda –
at Kew I am first hugged, then
crushed by the dragon Thames –
for she runs through everything
those days: they are a meadow
in my past that, now it is
swept by water, blooms
with orchids.

We married in
a meander of the Thames: lived
in an ox-bow, and walked
Waterloo Bridge mornings
at ten to the hour, below us
its broad black threat
of homelessness. You'd lived
in Hampton; I in Hounslow
had been drawn across
the dry conceptual heath
to your soft waters,
to the maze and stately home,
to the locks of my childhood . . .

The earliest memory I own
is of something dimly bright
warmly frightening at Boulter's
Lock − some bold confession
by the old gathered there
for a last day out, or
the moment of my own wakening:
I too will grow up
and grow old?

It took
the Nile to loose the river's
world serpent grasp
on our lives.
Our love
a long walk beneath Thames
willows grown too obese
to resist the spate, across
Petersham Meadows, past
riverside pub and private
jetty, upstream through endless
arches of ancient crossing.

Soon I will take our daughter
so she can know the Thames,
Sweet Thames, the silent
longing and searching of Isis.

ANNA ADAMS

(b. 1926)

The River Goddess in the A to Z

Blue contours of a living limb,
full curves suggesting hip and breast
abutting on right-angled, ruled
geometry of streets,
are fragments of the undivided
river-body, serpent-soul
of London, sliding past the ranks
of buildings on both river banks.

Reclined at ease, reflecting skies
far deeper than her bed, inhaling tides
brackish with North Sea salt, exhaling them
twice daily, dwindling then to puny size,
she knows in every molecule
of tributaries, river-mist, grey rain
and snowflakes vanishing in leaden skin
that she's an international local thing.

She makes her bed as she lies restlessly
on gravel; and, though British born,
she's an illegal immigrant. She's come
by cloud from Amazonian and African
and Asian waters. She has flown
to both the poles, circled the world's wide waist,
and is more cosmopolitan
than the great town she jigsaws, mirrors, joins.

There should be wisdom in her, reconciling
all that she knows with all that she has been:
rainforest, icefloe, flesh. If I look deep
and long into this liquid-muscled snake –
barred in by twenty bridges, who escapes
continuously – will my scale-dazzled eyes
see past her temporary local form
into her holy permanence? For she

66

led the procession that the earliest city
assembled on both banks to watch go by.
She mystifies the river-bordering park,
and is the wilderness at large in town,
stalking voluptuously by measured streets,
wearing the seamless sari of the world
dyed in our northern skies. She's grey and old,
gold and immortal: not to be controlled.

JEREMY HOOKER
(b. 1941)

from *City Walking, I*
(with Lee)

The old man
is full of stories.

In this place,
Julius Caesar's men
waded across the river,
and Saxons built a church
on what was then an island
of hard gravel, washed
by the river and surrounded
by miles of marsh.

The same from whose soil
Catherine Boucher's family
made their market garden –

Catherine, who, in this church,
married William Blake.

And here (our guide shows us
the vestry window) Turner
sat to paint clouds
and sunsets over the water –

where we can see tower blocks,
luxury flats, a marina,
a power station
that drives the Underground.

The old man too was married here,
twice; and his daughter
was christened, and wed . . .

As he talks, the empty church
fills silently with shadows.

It is a relief, then,
to walk on the shore
under the churchyard wall,
and look at houseboats, geese
in the water, and watch a tug
powering upriver, drawing
a barge with containers of waste.

At Battersea Bridge,
a heron flies over, mirrored
in a building of steel and black glass.

LAVINIA GREENLAW
(b. 1962)

River History

Even then the river carried cargo,
Saxon corn shipped to storehouses on the Rhine.
Taxes were paid in pepper and cloth by the Easterlings,
the German merchants trading from the Steelyard
demolished in the fire of 1666.
Wharves burned like touchpaper, packed
with resin, sulphur, pitch.
The daily catch between London and Deptford
was salmon, eel, smelt and plaice
but the Port Authority preferred to dine
at the Tavern on the best turtle soup in the City
as they argued the height of the wall to be built
against the Mudlarks, Plunderers and Peterboatmen,
intent on their nightly specialized percentage:
cloves from Zanzibar, mother-of-pearl,
tortoiseshell, South American iodine,
West Indian rum, the heavy iron bottles
of Spanish quicksilver, and, from Ivory House,
the occasional mammoth tusk unfrozen in Siberia.
The Empire expanded, cess-pits were banned,
water grew thick with steamships and sewage
and the docks pushed east out into the marshes,
breaking the horizon with a forest of cranes
that unloaded meat, cloth, tobacco and grain
from countries my school atlas still colours pink.
At the Crutched Friars Deposit Office records were kept
of ships in berth, noted daily
by a row of clerks crouched under gaslight
and seven-foot ceilings. Records were kept
of each member of the Union, the fight to be paid
a tanner an hour and not have to climb each day
on another's back and shout to be chosen.
There was always the army.
The Luftwaffe bombed Surrey Commercial Docks
for fifty-seven nights and the timber blazed

for more days than most people kept counting.
Even when every magnetic mine
had been located and cleared, there were dangers.
Centuries of waste had silted the river
till the water ran black over Teddington weir
and a bag of rubbish thrown from London Bridge
took six weeks to ride a dying current
out to the estuary. No swimming, no fish,
and those who fell in had to be sluiced out.
No ships, no work. The industry found itself
caught in the net of passing time,
watching mile after mile of dockland fill
with silence and absence. Land changed hands
in an estate agent's office, short-lease premises
with 'Upstream' and 'Downstream' carved above the doors.
Now the tidal traffic is a slow weekday flow of cars
channeled into streets built before cars were thought of.
They inch round corners, nudge against kerbs,
then settle tight packed against the pavement.
On Butler's Wharf, the only machinery
now in daily use is the tow-away truck:
cruising yellow lines, it pauses to hoist
the solid engineering of a badly parked BMW
into the air with illogical ease.
In Coriander Building, an agency
maintains the plants, the colour scheme is neutral
but the smell of new paint has yet to sink in,
like the spice that still seasons the air after rain.
A film crew arrives, on a costly location shoot
for *Jack the Ripper*. It's a crowded night.
Intent on atmosphere, they've cluttered the alleys
with urchins, trollops and guttersnipes
who drift to the waterfront when they're not working
and gaze across at the biggest, emptiest office block in Europe
and its undefendable, passing light.

RUTH PITTER
(1897-1992)

The Estuary

Light, stillness and peace lie on the broad sands,
On the salt-marshes the sleep of the afternoon.
The sky's immaculate; the horizon stands
Steadfast, level and clear over the dune.

There are voices of children, musical and thin,
Not far, nor near, there in the sandy hills;
As the light begins to wane, so the tide comes in,
The shallow creek at our feet silently fills:

And silently, like sleep to the weary mind,
Silently, like the evening after the day,
The big ship bears inshore with the inshore wind,
Changes her course, and comes on up through the bay,

Rolling along the fair deep channel she knows,
Surging along, right on top of the tide.
I see the flowery wreath of foam at the bows,
The long bright wash streaming away from her side:

I see the flashing gulls that follow her in,
Screaming and tumbling, like children wildly at play,
The sea-born crescent arising, pallid and thin,
The flat safe twilight shore shelving away.

Whether remembered or dreamed, read of or told,
So it has dwelt with me, so it shall dwell with me ever:
The brave ship coming home like a lamb to the fold,
Home with the tide into the mighty river.

THE POETS AND THE POEMS
Biographical notes by Anna Adams

(Joseph) Rudyard Kipling (1865-1936) was born in Bombay. Between the ages of six and twelve he was, with his sister Alice, boarded, unhappily, with a family at Southsea in England. During this time his father became the director of the Mayo School of Art and curator of the Lahore Museum. At thirteen the young Kipling was sent to the United Services College in Devon, and at seventeen he returned to India where he worked as a journalist and editor on papers in Lahore and Allahabad. He wrote articles, short stories and poems.

On his return to England in 1889 he was at once successful but also suffered a nervous breakdown. After his marriage he lived at first in America, then settled with his family in Sussex, but continued to travel widely.

He was intensely patriotic, and, in the spirit of his time, believed in the Empire. He also saw clearly the hard lives of British soldiers, and expressed their feelings in verses that echo their voices. He wrote the great hymn, 'Recessional', and, after the Great War which killed his only son, 'Gethsemane'.

It has to be remembered that the 'I' of a poem is not always the 'I' of the poet, (as Emily Dickinson said), and Kipling was obviously a great listener, and as able in his own way as Keats to practise 'negative capability'. In 'The River's Tale' he has become the tidal Thames, full of ancient knowledge, and physical love for his native land.

He was awarded the Nobel Prize for Literature in 1907. He influenced Bertolt Brecht, W. H. Auden, and, more recently, James Fenton.

William Dunbar (*c.*1460-*c.*1520) was Scottish, and belonged to the order of Observantine Franciscans. In his youth he travelled in France, then he became a priest at the court of James IV and was recognised as Laureate of the Scottish Court. He is credited with 101 poems in all. Much of his verse was humorous, but his 'Lament for the Makaris', and other religious poems, are as well known in England as this inspired flattery of medieval London, which is much anthologised.

Edmund Spenser (*c.*1552-99) was born in Smithfield, London, the son of a journeyman clothmaker. He was educated at Merchant Taylor's School with the help of money from public funds, and at Pembroke Hall, Cambridge. A gifted poet of wide scholarship, he claimed kinship with the great Spencers of Althorp in Northamptonshire, and they did not repudiate him.

The Faerie Queene, written in Ireland, is considered his greatest work, but the *Epithalamium* he wrote in celebration of his own marriage would be enough to be remembered by, as would the *Prothalamion* which was written on the occasion of the wedding of two daughters of the Earl of Worcester who were married from Essex House, by the Thames.

Spenser's early death, at forty-seven, was said at the time to be due to starvation, in London, after his flight from Ireland when his home there, Kilcolman Castle, was burned to the ground by an Irish uprising. One of his children died in the flames.

Sir John Denham (1615-69) was born in Dublin and educated at Trinity College, Oxford. He wrote his descriptive poem called 'Cooper's Hill' when he was twenty-seven. Dryden called it 'the exact standard of good writing' and Pope used it as a model for his early poem 'Windsor Forest'. Denham was a Royalist in the civil war, and from 1648 to 1652 found it advisable to live abroad. He wrote a famous elegy for his fellow poet Abraham Cowley.

John Dryden (1631-1700) was born of Puritan stock in Northamptonshire, and educated at Westminster School and Trinity College, Cambridge. While still a schoolboy he wrote a series of heroic stanzas to the memory of Oliver Cromwell. Later his sympathies were with the restored monarchy, which was as well, as he wrote for the stage for his living. In 1681 his satirical poem *Absalom and Achitophel* was a considerable success, running through nine editions in its first year. In 1685 Dryden became a Roman Catholic and his last decade was spent translating the Classics: Ovid, Lucretius, Theocritus and Virgil.

He died at Gerrard Street in London on May Day, 1700.

Alexander Pope (1688-1744). His first publication was in 1713, of *Windsor Forest*, which he began when he was sixteen or seventeen. He published the final version of *The Rape of the Lock* in 1714. This is a mock heroic epic based on a trivial event: William, 4th Baron Petre, had cut off a lock of Arabella Fermor's hair, and caused her disproportionate distress.

Pope later spent twelve years translating the works of Homer. Bentley, a contemporary critic, said of Pope's versions: 'Fine poems, Mr Pope, but you must not call them "Homer".'

Pope lived by the Thames at Twickenham and took great delight in his riverside garden.

Thomas Gray (1716-71) was born in London, the fifth and only surviving child of Philip Gray, a 'money scrivener'. His mother and her sister kept a small milliner's shop. Philip Gray was selfish and brutal, and his wife sent her son away to Eton College at her own expense. She also sought a separation from her husband. Her brother, William Antrobus, taught at Eton, and perhaps the care of this uncle atoned for the shortcomings of the father. Gray makes it clear in this 'Ode on a Distant Prospect of Eton College' that he was happy there, though he was prone to melancholy later in life.

William Blake (1757-1827) was born in Golden Square, Soho, London, the son of a hosier. He had no formal education but from the age of ten was sent to Par's Drawing School, in the Strand, and he was apprenticed to an engraver, James Basire, at the age of fifteen. For the rest of his life he earned his bread by this craft, and he also used his engraver's skill to reproduce his own imaginative designs, and – with the help of his wife Kate – produced illustrated books of poetry on his own press.

'London' is one of Blake's *Songs of Experience*, self-published in 1794, which followed the *Songs of Innocence* he had brought out in 1789. Twenty-four copies of the complete series of illustrated poems exist today.

'Why Should I Care for the Men of Thames?' is from the commonplace book used intermittently by Blake between 1793 and 1818. This book is known as 'The Rossetti Manuscript' because it was for some years in the possession of the poet/artist Dante Gabriel Rossetti.

William Wordsworth (1770-1850) was born at Cockermouth in Cumbria, and he lost his parents early. He went to school at Hawkshead, in the Lake District, and afterwards to Cambridge. As a young man he sympathised with the French Revolution, and he was also revolutionary in his verse. He rejected the artificiality of much eighteenth-century writing and wrote about the life ordinary people know in the world we all experience, in the common language of men speaking to men.

The sonnet composed 'Upon Westminster Bridge' is dated September 3, 1802. William and his sister Dorothy (1771-1855) had passed through London in July on their way to Calais where they were to meet Annette, by whom William had had a child as a result of his youthful sojourn in Paris when it was 'very heaven' to be alive.

In her journal about this journey, Dorothy wrote: '. . . on July 19th we arrived in London. . . . After various troubles and disasters we left London on Saturday morning at half past five or six, the 31st July (I have forgot which). We mounted the Dover coach at Charing Cross. It was a beautiful morning. The City, St Paul's, with the River and a multitude of little boats, made a most beautiful sight as we crossed Westminster Bridge. The houses were not overhung by their cloud of smoke and they were spread out endlessly, yet the sun shone so brightly with such a pure light that there was even something like the purity of one of nature's own grand spectacles.'

Thomas Hardy (1840-1928) is perhaps best known as a novelist, for he brought into being those powerful imaginary figures – Tess, Jude, Bathsheba Everdene, and so on – that continue to haunt and change human consciousness. Furthermore, his novels have been made into films and appeared on television, and you cannot make a film out of a poem. But Hardy wrote at least 900 poems, as well as the verse play *The Dynasts*, and is a major poet who has had a considerable influence on twentieth-century writers.

Much of his poetry is set in Dorset (Wessex), where he was born and spent most of his life, or in Cornwall where he did his courting. 'A Wife in

London' is one of a group of twelve war poems related to the Boer War, and it was first printed in book form in *Poems of the Past and the Present* in 1901.

Alice Meynell (1847-1922). 'The Visiting Sea' was published in her first collection, *Preludes*, in 1875, and included in *The Poems of Alice Meynell* (Oxford University Press, 1940). Intervening books were *Poems*, 1893; *Other Poems*, 1896; *Later Poems*, 1902; *Last Poems*, 1923.

Alice Meynell was married to Wilfrid Meynell, a prominent editor, and together they were friends of Francis Thompson.

Francis Thompson (1859-1907) was born in Preston, Lancashire, the son of a Catholic doctor. Rejected by the priesthood, he studied medicine in Manchester but failed to qualify. At twenty-six he left home and spent three years as an opium-addicted vagrant in London, until Wilfrid and Alice Meynell rescued him, published his poetry and found him lodgings, and refuges in monasteries in Sussex and Wales. His most famous poems are 'The Hound of Heaven' and 'The Kingdom of God'. He died of tuberculosis in 1907.

Oscar Wilde (1854-1900) was born in Dublin, the son of a successful surgeon, Sir William Wilde. His mother, Francesca Wilde, was herself a writer who published under the pen-name of 'Speranza'. At Magdalen College, Oxford, in 1878, Oscar won the Newdigate Prize for his poem 'Ravenna', but today he is remembered less as a poet than as a wit, story-teller, playwright, and also a pilloried and punished homosexual. His conversation and 'aestheticism' made him famous first; then his plays made him much more famous; but his appearance in the dock at the Old Bailey, and his resultant two-year sentence, made him notorious and put an end to his career, if not his writing, which continued under the name of Sebastian Melmoth.

The Ballad of Reading Gaol is probably his most-read poem these days. It would appear to have impressed the young Charles Hamilton Sorley before he wrote 'The River'.

'Symphony in Yellow' is a poem in aesthetic mode, with affinities to Whistler's painting.

After three years in exile, Oscar Wilde died in Paris on the 30 November 1900, aged forty-six.

Charles Hamilton Sorley (1895-1915) was a pupil at Marlborough College. In 1916, after his death in France, a book entitled *Marlborough and Other Poems* – some of great promise – was published and ran into several editions. 'The River', which seems to foresee his own death, was included in this volume.

Wilfred Owen (1893-1918) grew up in Shrewsbury and died fighting in France just before the Armistice. With Sassoon, Isaac Rosenberg and Edward Thomas, he is one of the foremost of the First World War poets, and possibly the greatest. Of his own war poems he said 'Above all I am not concerned

76

with Poetry', and 'The Poetry is in the pity.' Yet all his poems are made with skilful and imaginative art, having learned much from Keats and much from the Bible. 'Shadwell Stair' is a minor poem compared with Owen's angrily compassionate war poems. It is included in *The Collected Poems of Wilfred Owen*, first published by Chatto & Windus in 1963, and in *The Complete Poems and Fragments* (Oxford, 1983).

T. S. Eliot (1888-1965). 'The Fire Sermon' is the third part of *The Waste Land*, published in 1922. It is included in *The Complete Poems and Plays of T. S. Eliot* (Faber and Faber, 1969).

David Gascoyne (b. 1916) was born in Harrow, Middlesex. His first collection of poetry, *Roman Balcony and Other Poems*, was published in 1932 and a novel, *Opening Day*, in 1933. He was one of the earliest champions of Surrealism, publishing *A Short Survey of Surrealism* in 1935 and in the following year co-organising the London International Surrealist Exhibition. He lived in France in 1937-39, 1947-48 and 1953-64, and has been a distinguished translator of French poetry: in 1996 Enitharmon Press published his *Selected Verse Translations*. Among his other books are *Poems 1937-1942*, *A Vagrant and Other Poems* (1950) and *Night Thoughts* (1956). Enitharmon have also published his *Selected Poems* (1994), *Selected Prose 1934-1996* and *Encounter with Silence: Poems 1950*.

George Barker (1913-91), was first published in 1933. 'Battersea Park' was in his fourth collection, *Lament and Triumph*, 1940, and is included in his *Collected Poems*, edited by Robert Fraser and published by Faber and Faber in 1987.

Dylan Thomas (1914-53) was born in Swansea, South Wales. His father was a schoolmaster, and ambitious for his son, but Dylan failed to qualify for university entrance. He went to work as a reporter on the *South Wales Daily Post* while continuing to write poems in a back bedroom of his parents' house. His first small collection, *Eighteen Poems*, was published when he was twenty. *Twenty-five Poems* followed in 1936, and 'The Refusal to Mourn the Death, by Fire, of a Child in London' was in *Deaths and Entrances*, published in 1946.

Louis MacNeice (1907-63) was born in Northern Ireland, the son of a Protestant clergyman. He was one of the politically conscious, left-wing 'Thirties Poets' that included W. H. Auden, Christopher Isherwood, Cecil Day Lewis and Stephen Spender. He worked on a regular basis for the BBC. 'Charon' was a late poem, written in 1962, and its dark atmosphere seems to foresee his own death.

Stevie Smith (1902-71) was born in Hull, and had an absentee father. Her mother moved with her two young daughters and her sister, (Stevie's heroic

Aunt), to Avondale Road, Palmers' Green, London, where Stevie grew up and remained for the rest of her life. Her first book was *Novel on Yellow Paper* (1936), followed in 1937 by *A Good Time Was Had By All*, a collection of poems. *Over the Frontier* (1938), and *The Holiday* (1949), were subsequent novels, and she published eight more books of verse. She was at her most famous in the 1950s and '60s. 'The River God' was in *Harold's Leap* (1950). Probably her best-known poem is 'Not Waving but Drowning'.

U. A. Fanthorpe (b. 1929) was educated at Oxford and spent a number of years teaching. Then she worked as a clerk in a N.H.S. hospital, and it was from this experience that she gathered much of the material for her first collection, *Side Effects*, published by Harry Chambers/Peterloo Poets in 1978. 'Rising Damp' won third prize in the 1980 Arvon Foundation competition, and was included in her second collection, *Standing To*, from Peterloo Poets in 1982. A King Penguin *Selected Poems* came out in 1986. Her most recent collection is *Safe as Houses* (1995).

Derek Walcott was born in 1930 in St Lucia in the West Indies. He is now a citizen of Trinidad and Tobago and divides his time between Trinidad and the USA, where he teaches at Boston University. He was awarded the Queen's Gold Medal for Poetry in 1988 and the Nobel Prize for Literature in 1992. Among his most recent books are *Omeros* (Faber and Faber, 1990), *Selected Poetry* (1993) and *The Bounty* (1997).

Peter Redgrove was brought up in Kingston upon Thames, but now lives in Cornwall with his wife Penelope Shuttle. His most recent books of poetry are *Assembling a Ghost* (Cape, 1996) and *Orchard End* (Stride, 1996). A *New and Selected Poems* is due out from Cape in 1999. He co-authored, with Penelope Shuttle, their acclaimed book on menstrual poetics, *The Wise Wound*, a new edition of which is also due in 1999, from Marion Boyars. 'Staines Waterworks' was printed in his collection *My Father's Trapdoors* (Cape, 1994).

Andrew Motion was born in London in 1952 and educated at University College, Oxford. His poem 'Fresh Water' is from his eighth collection, *Salt Water*, published by Faber and Faber in 1997. He has written biographies of Larkin and Keats, and is currently Professor of Creative Writing at the University of East Anglia. He was appointed Poet Laureate in May 1999.

Lotte Kramer's 'After the Theatre' was included in her sixth collection, *Earthquake*, from Rockingham Press (1994), and her most recent books are *Selected and New Poems 1980-1997*, also from Rockingham, and a dual-text *Selected Poems* from the German publisher Brandes and Apsel; so the poetry of a child-refugee of the Thirties goes home in time for the Millennium.

Pauline Stainer's most recent book is *The Wound-dresser's Dream* (1996), her fourth collection from Bloodaxe. It was shortlisted for the Whitbread Prize. 'Pouring the Sand Mandala into the Thames' is to be included in the forthcoming *Parable Island*, otherwise it is as yet unpublished.

John Greening's poem 'The Thames' was first published in *Southfields*, a Scottish magazine. His latest poetry collection is *Nightflights: New and Selected Poems*, from Rockingham Press in 1998. Greening also writes plays and short stories, and is currently working with the composer Paul Mottram on a choral libretto for the Dunedin Consort.

Anna Adams' 'The River Goddess in the A to Z' was first published in *Poetry London Newsletter* in 1998. Her most recent collections are *Green Resistance: New and Selected Poems*, from Enitharmon Press, and *A Paper Ark* from Peterloo Poets, both in 1996.

Jeremy Hooker was born near Southampton in 1941. He has published ten collections of poems, the most recent being *Our Lady of Europe* (Enitharmon Press, 1997). He has also written and broadcast critical works about David Jones, John Cowper Powys, and *Writers in a Landscape*, published by the University of Wales Press.

He wrote 'City Walking (I)' in the summer of 1997 after a walk in London with the sculptor Lee Grandjean as companion and guide. The sequence forms part of a longer work called *Groundwork*, the second collaboration between Hooker and Grandjean. The first, *Their Silence a Language*, was published by Enitharmon Press in 1993.

Lavinia Greenlaw was born and grew up in London. 'River History' is included in her first collection from Faber and Faber, *Night Photograph*, published in 1993. Her second collection is *A World Where News Travelled Slowly* (Faber and Faber, 1997).

Ruth Pitter (1897-1992) was born in the East End of London. Her early poems were published in A. R. Orage's *New Age* while she was still at school. In 1920 her collection *First Poems* appeared. 'The Estuary' is from her ninth collection, *The Bridge*, published in 1945. She had received the Hawthornden Prize in 1937, and she won the Heinemann Award for Literature in 1954 and was the first woman to receive the Queen's Gold Medal for Poetry, in 1955. She was made a Companion of Literature in 1974 and C.B.E. in 1979. Her *Collected Poems*, published by Enitharmon Press in 1990 with an introduction by Elizabeth Jennings, were reissued in 1996.

She earned her living as a painter of furniture and trays, and after retiring from this she took up gardening, and found many poems in this activity; and she often appeared on the BBC Television *Brains Trust*. She died blind, aged 94, on 29 February 1992.

ACKNOWLEDGEMENTS

The publisher and editor gratefully acknowledge permission to reprint the following poems in this anthology:

GEORGE BARKER: 'Battersea Park' from *Lament and Triumph* (1940), reprinted in *Collected Poems*, edited by Robert Fraser (Faber and Faber, 1987), by permission of the publishers; T. S. ELIOT: 'The Fire Sermon' from *Collected Poems 1909-1962* (Faber and Faber, 1963), by permission of the publishers; U. A. FANTHORPE: 'Rising Damp' from *Standing To* (Peterloo Poets, 1982), by permission of the author; DAVID GASCOYNE: Extract from 'Megalometropolitan Carnival' from *Selected Poems* (Enitharmon Press, 1994), by permission of the author; JOHN GREEN-ING: 'The Thames', first published in *Southfields* magazine, by permission of the author; LAVINIA GREENLAW: 'River History' from *Night Photograph* (Faber and Faber, 1993), by permission of the author; JEREMY HOOKER: 'City Walking (I)', by permission of the author; LOTTE KRAMER: 'After the Theatre' from *Earthquake & Other Poems* (Rockingham Press, 1994), by permission of the author; LOUIS MacNEICE: 'Charon' from *Collected Poems* (Faber and Faber, 1979), by permission of David Higham Associates Ltd; ANDREW MOTION: 'Fresh Water' from *Salt Water* (Faber and Faber, 1997), by permission of the author and the Peters Fraser & Dunlop Group; RUTH PITTER: 'The Estuary' from *Collected Poems* (Enitharmon Press, 1996), by permission of Mark Pitter; PETER REDGROVE: 'Staines Waterworks' from *My Father's Trapdoors* (Cape, 1994), by permission of the author and David Higham Associates Ltd; STEVIE SMITH: 'The River God' from *Harold's Leap* (1950), reprinted in *The Collected Poems of Stevie Smith* (Penguin Books, 1989), by permission of James MacGibbon; PAULINE STAINER: 'Pouring the Sand Mandala into the Thames', by permission of the author; DYLAN THOMAS: 'The Refusal to Mourn the Death, by Fire, of a Child in London' from *Collected Poems 1934-1952* (J. M. Dent, 1952), by permission of David Higham Associates Ltd; DEREK WALCOTT: Extract from *Omeros* (Faber and Faber, 1990), by permission of the publishers.

Enitharmon Press would like to express warm thanks to Graham Crowley, Professor of Painting at the Royal College of Art, London, for his enthusiastic response to a commission to produce a Thames painting for reproduction on the cover.

We would also like to extend our thanks to Peter Black and his colleagues at the Hunterian Art Gallery, University of Glasgow, for very kindly providing photographs of Whistler's etchings to reproduce in the text.